KT-584-300

CLOTHES & CRAFTS IN

ANCIENT GREECE

Philip Steele

A ZOË BOOK

A ZOË BOOK

Devised and produced by
Zoë Books Limited
15 Worthy Lane
Winchester
Hampshire SO23 7AB
England

First published in Great Britain in 1998 by
Zoë Books Limited
15 Worthy Lane
Winchester
Hampshire SO23 7AB

A record of the CIP data is available from the British Library.

ISBN 1 86173 004 7

Printed in Belgium by Proost N.V.
Editor: Kath Davies
Design & Production: Sterling Associates
Illustrations: Virginia Gray

Photographic acknowledgments

The publishers wish to acknowledge, with thanks, the following photographic sources:

© AKG London / Erich Lessing / The Israel Museum, Jerusalem 17br, / Musée du Louvre, Paris 21t; C.M.Dixon 3, 4, 5t, 6b, 8t & b, 9l & r, 10b, 11, 14t, 15t & c, 16t, 17l, 18, 19tr, 20, 22t, 24t / The Archaeological Museum, Heraklion, Crete 6t, 7t & b / The Archaeological Museum, Istanbul 19tl / The Argos Museum, Greece 12b / The British Museum, London title page, 10t, 12t, 13, 16b, 19b, 21b, 22br, 23, 24b, 25b / The Delphi Museum, Greece 25t / The Ioannina Museum, Greece 15bl / The National Archaeological Museum, Athens / 14bl & r, 22bl / The National Museum, Copenhagen 5b.
Cover: C.M.Dixon top right, top left and centre / The National Archaeological Museum, Athens, bottom left / The Ioannina Museum, Greece, bottom right.

The publishers have made every effort to trace the copyright holders, but if they have inadvertently overlooked any, they will be pleased to make the necessary arrangement at the first opportunity.

CONTENTS

INTRODUCTION

▲ A sailing ship and dolphins come to life on this cup. It was made in Greece about 530 BC. Colonists and traders shipped Greek craft items across the Mediterranean and the Black Sea.

Greece is a land of mountains, islands and blue seas, in southern Europe. It was here that several great civilizations grew up between about 2000 and 196 BC. Greek ideas, arts and **craft** skills have inspired the rest of the world ever since these ancient times.

The great **Minoan** civilization began in Crete about 5000 years ago. Beautiful pottery, metalwork and Minoan paintings can still be seen in museums today. The **Mycenaeans** of southern Greece traded with the Minoans. The Mycenaeans went on to become the most powerful people in the Aegean region. Their wars with the city of Troy, in Asia Minor, passed into legend. They gave pride of place to their craftworkers, who produced fine jewellery, pottery and weapons. The Mycenaeans lived in hilltop **citadels** in southern Greece.

The most important period in ancient Greece began after 700 BC. At that time, small islands and **city-states** on the

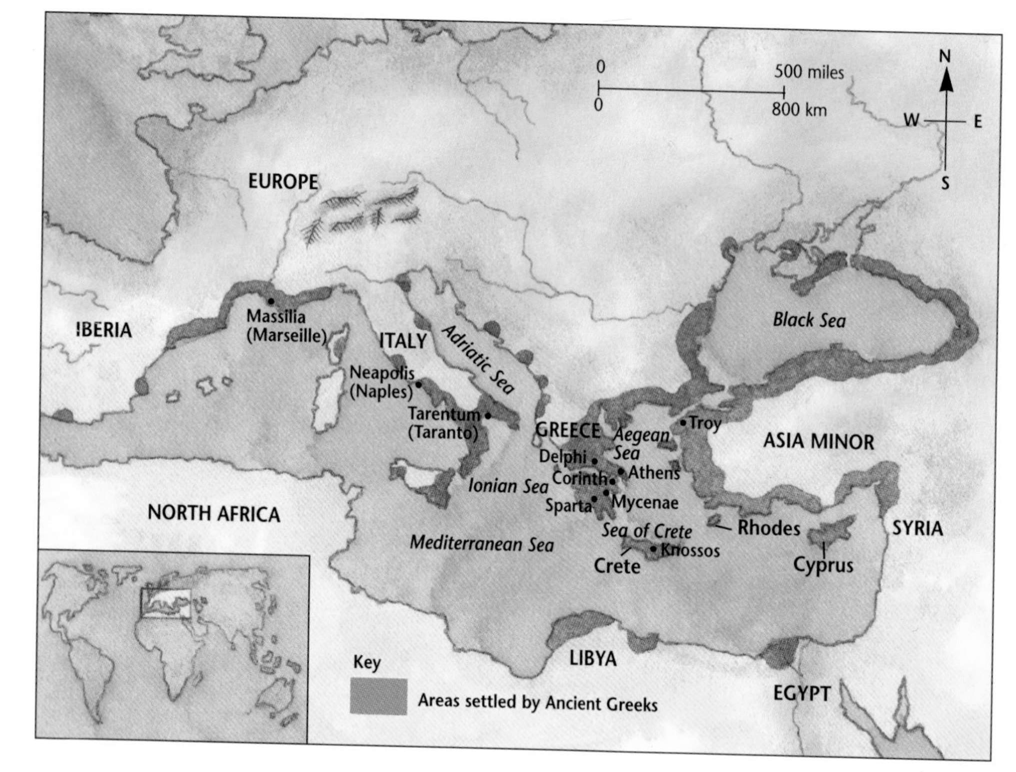

◀ The lands around the Aegean Sea lay at the centre of the Greek world. The Greeks were never united in a single country. They fought against each other as much as against their common enemies.

The Ancient Greeks never had a great European empire like that of the Romans. However, they were great seafarers and explorers. From about 750 BC onwards, many Greeks left their mountain homes and rocky islands. They set up new trading **colonies** overseas.

◀ The Parthenon still stands on the Acropolis, the rocky hill above the city of Athens. This beautiful temple to the Greek goddess Athene was completed in about 432 BC, during the '**golden age**' of Athens. It was decorated with fine marble carvings.

mainland became wealthy and powerful. Within 250 years, cities such as Athens, Corinth and Sparta were home to great thinkers, politicians, writers, architects, artists and craftworkers. In 338 BC, the northern Greek kingdom of Macedonia defeated the city-states.

Between 334 and 323 BC, the Macedonian ruler of Greece, Alexander the Great, founded a new **empire** which eventually stretched from Egypt to India. The influence of Greek artists and craft workers spread far and wide. It was particularly strong in the lands ruled from Rome. The Roman army defeated the Macedonian Greeks in 196 BC.

Across blue seas

The ancient Greeks had few natural resources, so they had to buy in, or **import**, grain and other raw materials. They sold, or **exported**, wine, olive oil and pottery to other countries.

- Egypt provided a reed called papyrus for making paper and rope.
- Libya provided elephant tusks for ivory.
- The Black Sea ports exported timber.
- Syria and the Middle East provided perfumes.
- Asia Minor provided gold.
- The Mediterranean island of Elba exported iron, while the mines of Cyprus produced copper.
- Tin came from distant Cornwall, in Britain.
- Silver was mined in Spain and at home in Greece.

▶ A furniture maker from the Greek region of Boeotia goes to work with his bow saw. This model dates from about 500 BC.

GREEK CRAFTS

Minoan magic

Crete is a beautiful Mediterranean island, with high mountains, deep caves and a rocky coast.

By about 2000 BC, several towns had grown up on the island and splendid palaces had been built in the north of Crete. Greek legends say that Knossos was the home of a powerful king called Minos, which is why the civilization of ancient Crete is called 'Minoan'.

The Minoans worshipped the **Earth Mother** and other gods and goddesses. Their holy, or sacred, symbol was a double-bladed axe called a *labrys* and their sacred animal was the bull. They traded with the ancient Egyptians, who influenced Minoan arts and crafts.

▲ This fine wall painting from Knossos shows a priest-king. He wears a brief loincloth and a plumed head dress. Cretan men wore loincloths, leather belts and high boots. The women wore dresses with full skirts, tight bodices and bare breasts. Men and women wore their hair long and curled.

◀ In 1900 a British archaeologist called Sir Arthur Evans began to dig up, or **excavate**, the site of Knossos. The dig uncovered a magnificent palace which had been rebuilt after an earthquake in about 1700 BC. The site included a throne room, royal apartments, courtyards, craft workshops and storerooms for goods to be exported.

▶ A Minoan craftworker made this gold **pendant** at some time between 1700 and 1450 BC. It shows two bees and a honeycomb. Crete was a centre for work in metals and precious stones. At the royal court, women wore necklaces, gold earrings and strings of pearls in their hair.

The **potter's wheel** was used on Crete as early as 1900 BC and Minoan pottery was an important export.

People who study the things which other people made or built long ago are called **archaeologists**. They have discovered Minoan wood-working tools and workshops where jewellery, ivory, bronze and copper items were made. Workers wove **textiles** and made soft leather from deer hides.

The world of ancient Crete was shown in vivid wall paintings, or **frescoes**, which survive today. They show dolphins, birds, **griffins** and lilies, and acrobats vaulting over the horns of bulls.

The Minoan world declined after 1450 BC. A massive volcanic eruption blasted apart the nearby island of Thira (Santorini). Earthquakes and shock waves caused huge waves which flooded the Cretan coast. The palaces caught fire and fell into ruin.

▼ Massive **earthenware** jars were found at Knossos. They were made for storing foods. This one is decorated with a *labrys* design. It is about 3400 years old.

A craftsman who aimed too high

An ancient Greek legend tells of Daidalos, a brilliant craftsman and inventor from Athens, who built a maze called the Labyrinth for King Minos of Crete. Daidalos, imprisoned by Minos, tried to fly away from Crete by building wings of wax and feathers. However, his son, Ikaros, flew too close to the Sun. The wax melted in his wings and he fell into the sea.

Warriors of the citadel

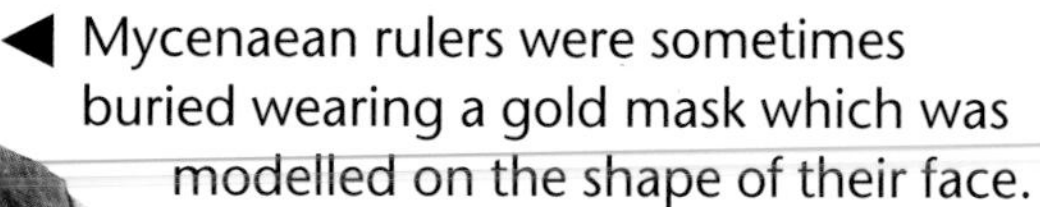

◀ Mycenaean rulers were sometimes buried wearing a gold mask which was modelled on the shape of their face. The custom probably came from the Egyptians. This mask was excavated in 1876 by a famous German archaeologist called Heinrich Schliemann. He thought it was the mask of Agamemnon, the king of Mycenae who led the Greeks to war against Troy. In fact, the mask is much older than the Trojan wars.

The Cretans of the Minoan period traded with the peoples who lived on the mainland of Greece. These included the people living around heavily fortified citadels such as Mycenae, Tiryns, Argos, Dendra, Kastro and Pylos in the **Peloponnese**. These Mycenaeans worshipped various gods and goddesses, including the all-powerful sky-god Zeus. The Mycenaean civilization developed from about 1900 BC. It reached its peak when the Mycenaeans took control of the island of Crete after the disasters of 1450 BC.

The bearded Mycenaean warriors wore bronze armour lined with leather. They

▼ The citadel of Mycenae was at its most powerful about 3200 years ago. Above one of its gates are two great lions carved in stone.

▼ Heinrich Schliemann's wife Sophie models beautiful jewellery. It was made for a princess of Troy more than 3000 years ago.

▲ A Mycenaean potter made this storage jar with an octopus design, about 3400 years ago. The Mycenaeans traded widely in pottery – with Egypt and Libya, the Middle East and the lands around the Black Sea, Italy and possibly France and Spain.

travelled in horse-drawn chariots and carried bronze daggers, swords, long spears and huge, hide-covered shields shaped like figures-of-eight. Their warships sailed the Aegean Sea, and there were Mycenaean colonies on Rhodes and Cyprus. However, by 1100 BC Mycenaean power was destroyed by wars.

The citadels of Mycenaean Greece were skilfully built of massive stones set in clay, topped by battlements of mud. There were arches and gateways of carved stone.

Within the walls were palaces, courtrooms and treasuries for storing gold and jewels. There were smithies and workshops for producing bronze, silver, gold and carved ivory.

Like the Cretans, the Mycenaeans decorated their palace walls with paintings. Styles of art and pottery were greatly influenced by those of Crete.

▼ This bronze dagger blade is inlaid with gold and silver. It shows scenes of a lion hunt. Lions still lived in Greece 3500 years ago.

'Rich in gold ...'

Heinrich Schliemann (1822-90) was a German businessman who had a dream.

He had read the exciting stories about the wars between the Mycenaean Greeks and the Trojans, as told by the Greek poet Homer in the tenth century BC. Most historians believed that these were little more than tales. Schliemann claimed that the tales were true.

Schliemann found the site of ancient Troy in 1871. He began to uncover the fabulous treasures left in the graves of Mycenae, which date back to about 1600 BC. Homer had described Mycenae as 'rich in gold'. Schliemann proved that this was true.

Classical Greece

The Mycenaean age ended with bitter wars, invasions from the north and movements of peoples across Greece and southwest Asia. It was not until the 700s BC that Greece became more peaceful. This was the age of growing trade and of new Greek colonies overseas. Crafts were influenced by Egyptian and Syrian styles.

▼ The masons carved **columns** in various styles. The Doric style was plain and simple, and was widely used on the Greek mainland and in the Italian colonies. The Ionic style was more elegant, with a curly top piece, or **capital**, to help support the roof. Capitals were often carved with leaves, flowers, heads or swirling patterns. This capital in the Ionic style is from the Erechtheion in Athens.

▲ The outside of the Parthenon was decorated with a carved stone **frieze** which was 160 metres long. It showed the great festival held in honour of the goddess Athene.

Between 499 and 479 BC, the small city-states of Greece defied neighbouring Persia, the super-power of the day. This mighty empire was ruled by all-powerful kings. In Athens, however, the Greeks were experimenting with an exciting new idea – government by a public assembly. This was the beginning of **democracy**. The new political freedoms were matched by a spirit of freedom and beauty in the arts and crafts.

Carved in stone

The ancient Greeks were not only great architects, they were brilliant carvers of stone, or masons. Today, about 2450 years after the golden age of classical Greece,

▲ The Erechtheion is one of the most impressive Greek temples. It was built on the Acropolis in Athens. Columns of female figures called *caryatids* supported the roof.

the Greek landscape is scattered with the ruins of beautiful temples and theatres.

Stonemasons decorated the buildings with some of the finest statues and friezes ever carved. In the 700s BC, statues were often stiff and formal, but over the years Greek sculptors learned to make the stone almost come alive.

The stone was often marble, quarried from Mount Pentelikos and Mount Hymettos in Attica, and from the islands of Paros and Naxos. Much of this stone, which now gleams white in the sun, would have been painted for dramatic effect.

Who did the hard work?

Who built the Erechtheion between 435 and 407 BC? A carving, or inscription, tells us about the workforce in 408 – 407 BC.

- There were 24 Athenian citizens – architects, administrators, masons, sculptors, wood-carvers and tilers.
- There were 42 *metics*. These were free men but were not Athenian born and bred, so they had no vote in the public assemblies. They too included skilled workers.
- Twenty slaves were employed, not only as labourers but also as masons and carpenters.
- Free, skilled workers could earn one ***drachma*** a day, but the slaves earned nothing, which meant a healthy profit for the builders. Athens may have been a democracy, but its economy depended on slave labour.

Classic terracotta

Terracotta was originally an Italian term meaning 'baked earth'. It is sometimes called earthenware. Ancient Greek craftworkers used this plain, baked clay for everyday items such as roofing tiles or children's toys. They also used it to make fine works of art, such as small statues, figurines and decorative friezes on buildings.

◀ This terracotta figure is of a comic actor. He is wearing a mask which shows that he is playing the part of a slave.

Vases and dishes

The potters' district in ancient Athens, Kerameikos, gave its name to our word 'ceramics' – fine, fired pottery.

Athenian potters used local, red clay and worked on potters' wheels. Quality clay also came from Cape Kolias, Corinth and Knidos.

People used pottery containers for carrying and storing wine and water, for storing olive oil and foodstuffs and to hold perfumes and make-up, or cosmetics. There were many different designs and shapes.

Until about 700 BC, most vases were decorated with shaped, or geometric, patterns.

▶ This detail from a pottery vase shows a man and a horse surrounded by geometric patterns. The vase comes from Argos and dates from before 700 BC.

Asian and Egyptian designs such as griffins and lions were popular until a new Greek style developed. This included scenes and figures painted as black **silhouettes** on a red clay background. In the 400s BC, red figures appeared on a black background.

The pictures on these vases give us clues about how the Greeks lived, dressed and enjoyed themselves, about their warriors, sporting champions and their religious beliefs.

▲ A detail from a drinking cup, made in about 550 BC, is decorated with black and white figures on a red background. The picture is of a hunter and his dog.

Broken shards

People usually wrote by scratching on wax-covered boards. However, bits of broken pottery, or shards, were also used as notebooks or for sending messages.

- When the Athenian assembly met to exile any citizens, their names were written on these shards, called *ostraka* in Greek.
- We still use the word 'ostracize', when somebody loses favour with the public.

◀ Pictures of griffins decorate this wine jug, which was made in Corinth in about 600 BC.

Working in metal

Smiths and metalworkers were important in ancient Greece. Greek traders imported ores of copper, gold, tin, silver and iron from around the Mediterranean and as far away as the British Isles. The silver mines at Laurion in Attica, worked by slave gangs, provided the wealth that made Athens powerful.

▼ This commanding figure is Zeus, the chief god of the Greeks and the ruler of the heavens. It was cast in bronze in about 460 BC. The Romans stole the figure from its temple, and dropped it into the sea off Cape Artemision. It is now in the National Museum at Athens.

◀ A bronze figure of a *hoplite*, which shows his crested helmet and shield.

An important part of the smith's skills involved making tools, armour and weapons. A young Spartan footsoldier, or *hoplite*, from a good family had to provide his own equipment when he marched off to war. He had a bronze helmet with a horse-hair crest, perhaps a bronze cuirass (hinged armour to protect the chest and the back) and greaves (armour to fit around the shins). Weapons of the 500s and 400s BC included short swords and spears with iron blades.

Kitchen pots and pans as well as grand vases, jugs and ladles for serving wine at banquets were produced by metalworkers.

▶ This bronze figure of the goddess Athene dates from about 500 BC. It shows her fully armed for war.

They made fittings for wooden furniture, polished mirrors and all kinds of jewellery.

Some of the finest works of art produced in ancient Greece are statues and small figures. They were made of bronze, sometimes inlaid with silver and copper. There are figures of charioteers, athletes, soldiers, wealthy citizens, gods and goddesses. Huge statues were placed in many temples. The wooden statue of Athene in the Parthenon was nearly 12 metres high, cased in gold and carved ivory.

▼ Bronze was used to make all kinds of vases, jugs and wine jars, as well as pots and pans for the kitchen.

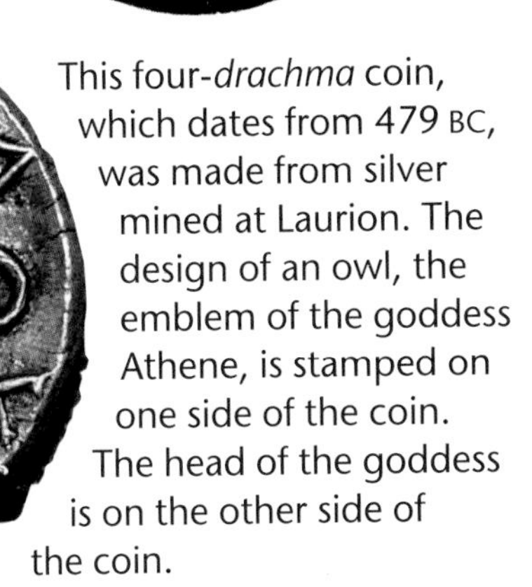

This four-*drachma* coin, which dates from 479 BC, was made from silver mined at Laurion. The design of an owl, the emblem of the goddess Athene, is stamped on one side of the coin. The head of the goddess is on the other side of the coin.

Hephaistos the smith

Metalworking was so important to ancient peoples that it was sometimes thought of as magic, or the work of the gods.

- Hephaistos, the Greek god of fire, protected smiths and metalworkers. It was said that his furnaces on the sacred slopes of Mount Olympus were fired by twenty bellows.
- Hephaistos, according to the myth, made the bronze armour of Achilles, the Greek hero of the Trojan wars.

Inside the home

Most Greek houses were built of mud bricks and plaster. They had two storeys, small, shuttered windows (without glass) and terracotta roof tiles. Country houses stood amongst olive groves and fields and were surrounded by a stone wall. Town houses were often in crowded alleys and were sometimes workshops too.

Inside Greek houses, the rooms opened on to a central courtyard. Here there might be a tree, herbs or vines, a well, an open hearth for cooking and a stone altar to the gods. The women's rooms contained a weaving frame, or loom, and cradles for babies. The dining room was for men only – banquets were usually all-male.

◀ There are two fine wooden chairs in this picture on a painted vase.

By today's standards, there was little furniture. Wood was precious and some of it had to be imported. There were low couches and tables with decorative metal fittings, chairs, stools and simple beds. Wood does not survive well, so most of

▼ Guests at banquets lay sideways on low couches to eat. This bronze figure of a dinner guest, dates from about 530 BC.

our information about classical Greek furniture comes from paintings and friezes. These show that furniture was often elegant and well made.

Musical instruments

Music was popular in the home, at banquets, at religious festivals, in the theatre, and even in wars, as soldiers were piped into battle.

- The most finely crafted instruments were lyres. They were made from wood, ivory and tortoise-shell, and fitted with strings of animal gut.
- Pipes, or *auloi*, were carved from woods such as sycamore. The mouthpiece was fitted with a reed.
- Dancers might be accompanied by castanets, small cymbals made of bronze, drums and tambourines.

▼ Indoor lighting came from oil lamps fitted with slow-burning **wicks**. Most oil lamps were made of terracotta. Some, like this one, were made of bronze.

▲ This stone carving shows a lyre being played.

Hellenistic crafts

In 338 BC, the northern Greeks of Macedonia, under King Philip II, defeated the armies of Athens and Thebes at the battle of Chaeronea. The age of the independent city-states was over. In 336 BC, Alexander, Philip's young son, became ruler of all Greece. Two years later, he began his conquest of western Asia.

Alexander the Great was not simply a brilliant soldier. He was interested in the **cultures** of the peoples in his new empire. The Greek world opened up to new influences and ideas and in turn Asia opened up to the west. Even today, Pakistani boys may be given the name Sikander (Alexander). After Alexander died, his vast empire was divided amongst his family and rival generals.

▲ Pergamon was a Greek city in Asia Minor. Its theatre, shown here, can still be seen today. Its library, founded by Attalus I (ruled 241-197 BC), is said to have contained more than 200,000 scrolls. The kings of the Hellenistic period competed with each other to found centres of learning and culture.

The Greek – or Hellenistic – way of life influenced Egypt and Asia, the Greeks' Italian colonies and the powerful new city of Rome. Beautiful new cities, such as Priene in Asia Minor, were carefully planned and well laid out on a **grid** pattern. This was an age of advances in science and technology, and of the first great libraries, the most famous of which was at Alexandria.

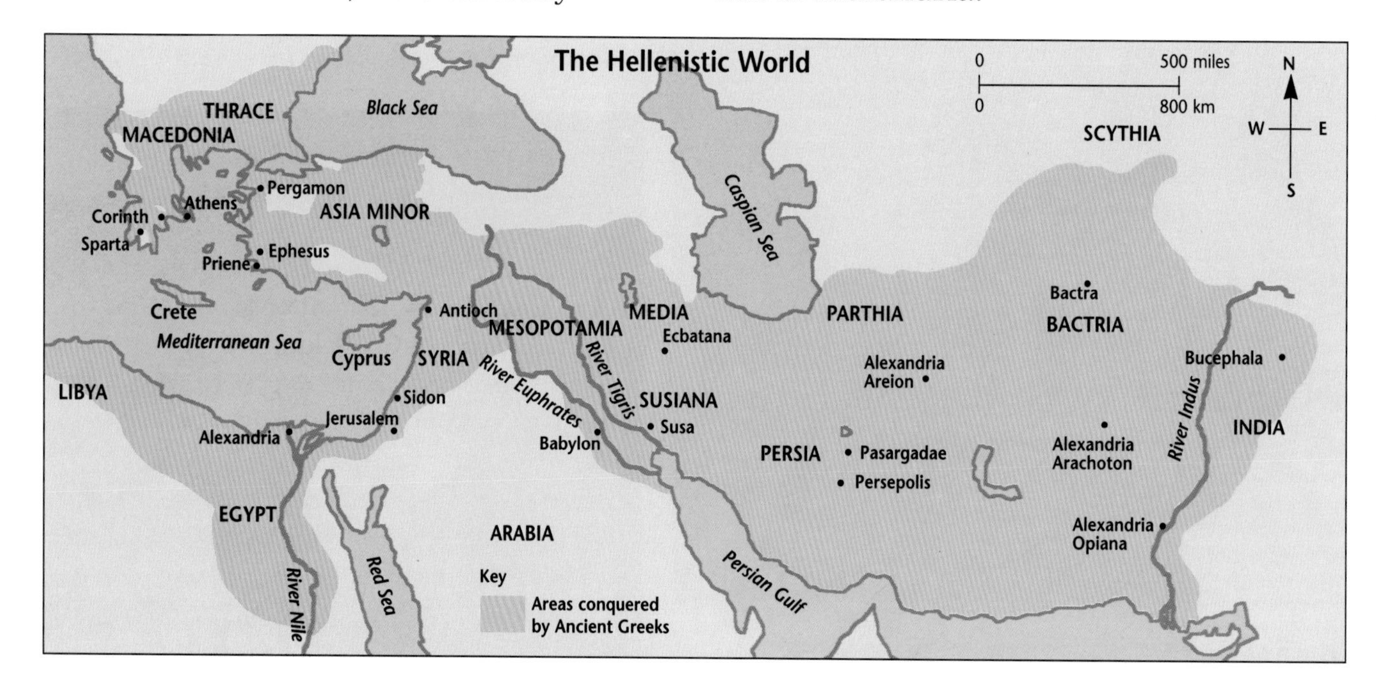

▲ Alexander's deeds passed into legend. Here they are shown on a frieze from a stone coffin case, or sarcophagus. It dates from about 325-300 BC, and was found in the royal cemetery at the Mediterranean city of Sidon. The scenes of hunting and warfare are extremely realistic.

Hellenistic craftworkers used a wide range of raw materials and worked in different traditions. They produced gold jewellery, glass, carved stones and pottery. The style of sculptures and carvings became more and more realistic.

▼ Hellenistic art was very realistic as you can see from these two figures made from terracotta. They were made in Myrina, Asia Minor in about 100 BC.

▲ This ornate gold necklace was made in the Hellenistic style. It was found in the tomb of a priestess at Tarentum, a Greek colony in southern Italy. It dates from 340 BC.

Greek design and decoration often blended with Asian and Egyptian subjects or styles. For example, a **sardonyx** dish from the age of Cleopatra, a Greek queen of Egypt, shows the ancient Egyptian gods – but they are carved to look like Greek gods.

Paper and parchment

The libraries of the Hellenistic world were filled with scrolls, not books.

- The paper for the scrolls was mostly made from papyrus, a reed that grows along the banks of the River Nile. The ancient Egyptians stripped the reed stems, hammered them together and smoothed the surface. Under the rule of Greek kings, Egypt continued to be a centre of paper-making.
- People also made writing material from the skin, or hide, of sheep, goats or calves. It was called parchment, a word which comes from the name Pergamon. This Hellenistic city was a centre of parchment production.

CLOTHES AND FASHION

Weaving and textiles

Wool was the most important material for the ancient Greeks. Textiles, including wall hangings, blankets, cushions and clothing, were all produced at home by the women and the household slaves. Some women also sold woollen thread, or yarn, in the market.

The wool was first washed and combed, or carded, to untangle it. It was then wrapped around a split, or cleft, stick called a distaff, from which it was teased out with the fingers. A whirling weight called a drop spindle, made of wood, bone or bronze, was used to spin the wool **fibres** into thread. Finally, the thread was woven into textiles on looms, which were usually upright wooden frames with weighted **warp** threads.

▲ This picture on an Athenian wine jug shows a woman holding a distaff. The yarn would be spun by a twirling spindle.

◀ These sheep are on the western slopes of Mount Parnassos. Flocks of sheep like this grazed the hillsides of ancient Greece. Their fleeces were shorn on the farms and estates.

Between about 550 and 480 BC, linen cloth became more popular than wool. It was made from a plant called **flax** which was mostly grown in Egypt. Light linen was cooler and more comfortable to wear in hot weather, although wool was still worn in winter. Greek warriors soon used tougher linen in battle, instead of the heavy bronze cuirass.

The Hellenistic period saw the introduction of cotton and fine silks from the east. The Greek island of Kos became the centre of a silk industry, with mulberry trees planted there to feed the **silkworms**. Such rich textiles would have been frowned upon by the Greeks' ancestors, who passed laws against luxurious dress. Textiles used for clothes were dyed but were rarely embroidered.

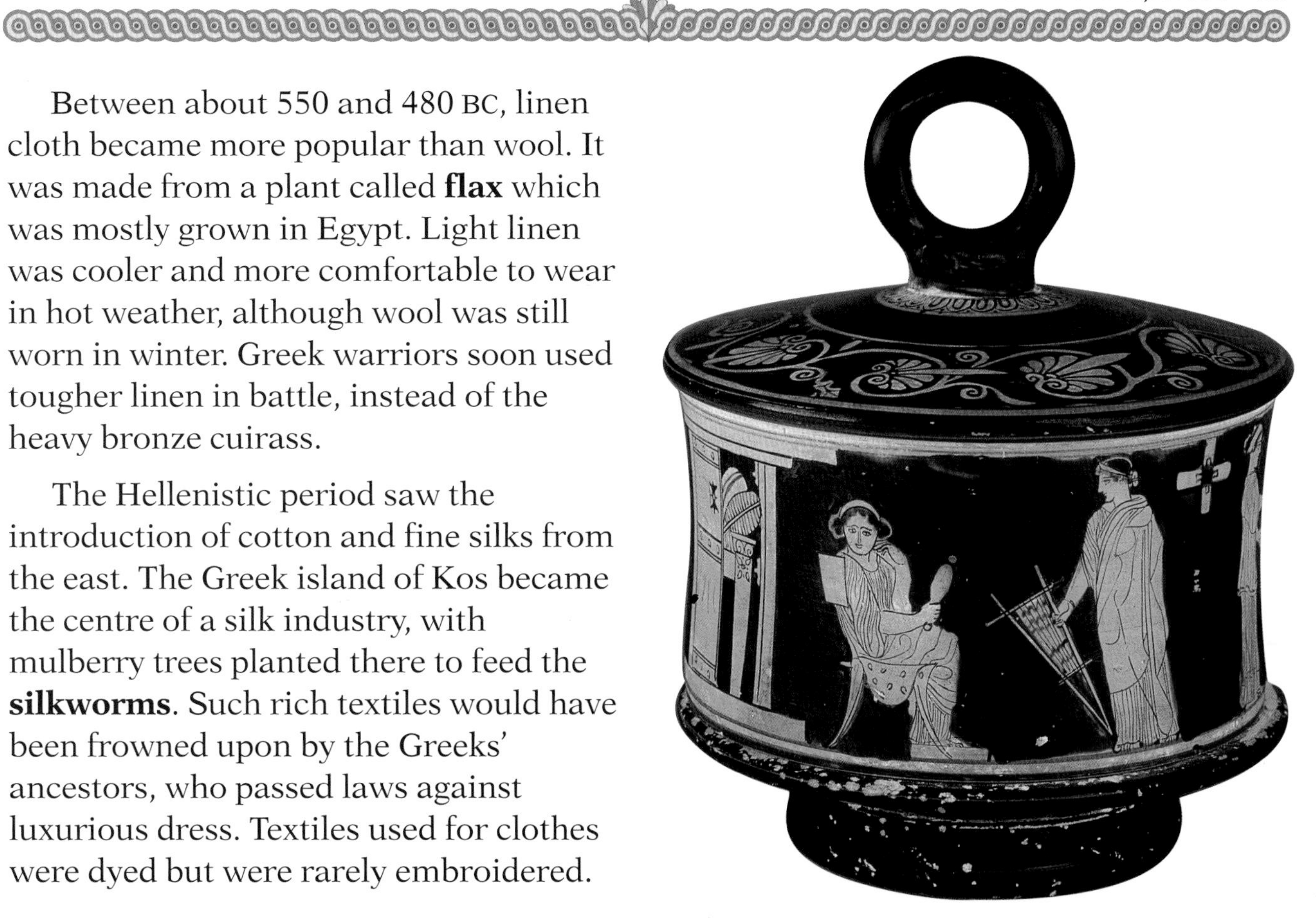

▲ This powder jar was made about 430 BC. It shows Greek women spinning and weaving. The warp threads hang down from the weaving frame. The cross-threads, or **weft** runs across the frame.

▼ An Athenian vase made around 450 BC shows a woman handing a red-dyed cloak to her maid.

Snails and insects

Most Greek textiles were white. The chemicals we use for dyeing cloth today were unknown in the ancient world. At that time, dyes came from natural sources.

- All kinds of herbs, leaves, barks and roots provided vegetable dyes.
- A popular purple dye came from a kind of sea snail called murex. It was produced at the Mediterranean city of Tyre. This city came under Greek influence in the Hellenistic period.
- A red dye came from the dried, scaly bodies of an insect called the kermes. It lives on oak trees in the Mediterranean area.

Dress for men and women

In the ancient world, fashions changed more slowly than they do today. There were times when simple styles were popular and there were also periods of luxury. The men and women of Sparta always preferred simple, practical fashions.

Working people, slaves and children usually wore short tunics which allowed greater freedom of movement. Athletes and gymnasts usually trained and performed naked.

◀ Spartan girl athletes wore short tunics. The Athenians thought that the Spartan women were most 'unladylike'.

Underclothes, when they were worn, were simply pieces of cloth wrapped around the body. Both men's and women's clothes were based on a tunic design. The women wore a long woollen dress, or *peplos*, gathered with a belt at the waist. It could be worn over one shoulder or secured at both shoulders with brooches or pins.

▲ Dress pins were usually made of bronze and were about 45 cm long. This Mycenaean pin is made of silver with an ornate golden head.

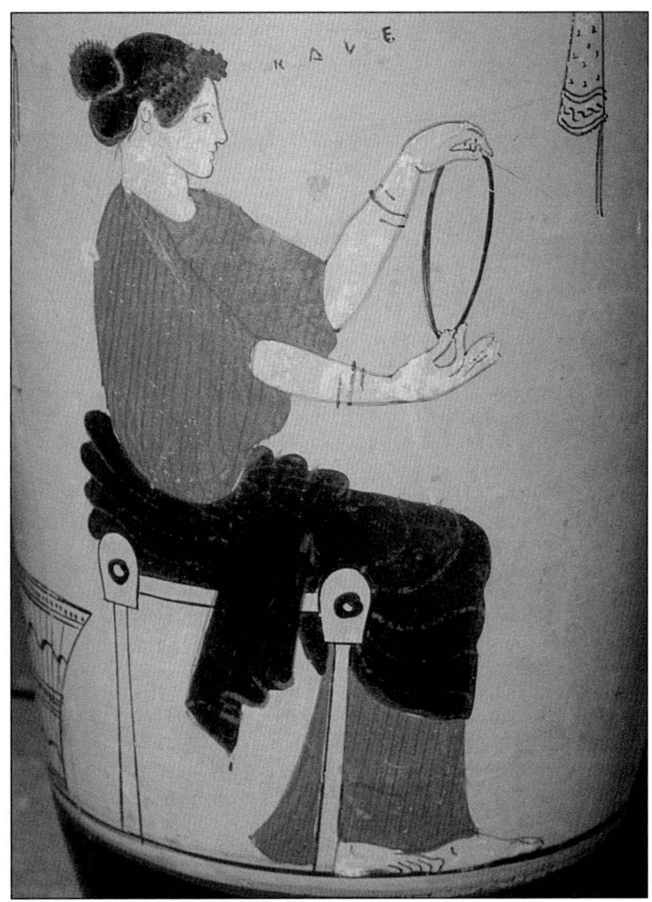

▼ A woman admires her *chiton* and hairstyle in a mirror.

By the 550s BC, a new, eastern-style tunic was becoming more popular with both men and women. Called the *chiton*, it was joined across the shoulders and so needed no pins. It was usually made of linen. The fashion could be varied by the way it was folded and draped. In the 400s BC, many men stopped wearing long tunics and wore a full cloak, the *himation*. The most famous cloak worn in ancient Greece was scarlet, and was worn by all Spartan warriors as a sign of their bravery.

Sunhats and sandals

- In classical Greece, men and women wore sandals of leather thongs. Men sometimes wore short or long boots. People often went barefoot in the home.
- Women sometimes covered their heads with a veil or cloak. Men were often bare-headed, but there were hats made of straw, wool or fur to provide shade from the sun or protection from the weather. These included skull-caps worn under helmets, broad-brimmed sunhats, conical hats and bonnets.

▶ In pictures, Greek gods and goddesses were often shown wearing ordinary Greek dress. This scene was painted on a drinking cup more than 2400 years ago. You can see the graceful folds of the woman's *chiton*.

Looking beautiful

Greek women usually let their hair grow long. In Athens they knotted it behind the head, while in Sparta they wore it in a pony-tail. On a girl's wedding day, locks of her hair were sometimes cut off and offered to the gods. Hair was also cut short as a sign of mourning, or as a mark of slavery.

Over time, fashionable women's hairstyles became more and more complicated. Women wore gold and silver headdresses, bands of bronze, ribbons and nets in their curls and ringlets. Wigs and false hairpieces were popular.

Men cared about their hair as much as women did. Early styles included curls, plaits and long hair held back with a

▼ These gold ornaments were worn on the chest. They show Artemis, the goddess of wild animals and hunting.

▲ A scent bottle made in Rhodes in about 575 BC is shaped like a fashionable lady. She wears make-up and a necklace.

The right complexion

In the hot sun, working men's and women's skin soon became tanned. Greek women of high birth rarely left home, so pale skin was prized as a sign of wealth.

- Some people used lead powder to make their skin paler. This was actually very poisonous.
- Women also used eyeliner and blusher, and oils, lotions and scents made from roses, herbs and **myrrh**.

metal tie. Later, people wore their hair short, with different partings. Beards were popular in the early days, but by the time of Alexander most men were clean shaven. Both men and women dyed, oiled and perfumed their hair. They used combs carved from ivory or bone.

Craftworkers in ancient Greece produced fine jewellery. There were gold earrings, delicate necklaces, rings and sparkling jewels.

▲ This charioteer wears his hair short and curled. The bronze figure comes from Delphi.

▼ These terracotta figures show two women playing the game of knucklebones. One wears her hair long, the other wears it gathered under a headdress.

FESTIVALS AND HOLIDAYS

Festivals played an important part in Greek life. They were usually held to honour the gods and goddesses, and often included sacrifices of animals and secret ceremonies. Many festivals involved music, feasting and drinking, public processions or chariot races. Home life also had its special joyful or solemn occasions, marking childhood, marriage and death.

The greatest Athenian festival was the *Panathenaea*, held each year. The whole city joined in the procession up to the Acropolis. People carried a symbolic gift of new clothes for the goddess Athene.

Two Greek traditions which influence the world today started out as religious festivals. One was the Olympic Games, first recorded in 776 BC but probably much older. This was such a sacred occasion that even wars stopped while the games were in progress. Long jump, horse-racing, foot races, javelin and discus-throwing were all popular events. The prizes awarded were simple crowns of leaves, or wreaths. However, when a victorious competitor returned home there were lavish rewards, feasting and celebrations.

Another festival tradition produced Greek drama. The first great **tragedies** and **comedies** were played at public festivals to honour the god Dionysos.

Toys for the gods

Greek girls and boys played all sorts of games and had many toys. When they became teenagers, a ceremony was held to mark their coming of age. Their toys were taken away and dedicated to the god Apollo or the goddess Artemis. Make a Greek toy from clay. Follow these instructions to make a toy goose from clay, or you could make a horse if you prefer.

You will need: • modelling clay that hardens • paints

1. Make a model goose on a base, like the one shown here. Use clay that hardens.

2. Make a rider and place it on the goose's back.

3. Paint the goose white with an orange beak. Give the rider a blue tunic and a red cap.

A painting for a palace

The Cretans made beautiful wall paintings on plaster. They included celebrations and feasts at the palace of Knossos. The paintings show cupbearers bringing jars of wine to the guests, and acrobats leaping over bulls. You can make your own wall painting or frieze.

You will need: • a long piece of card • tracing paper • pencils, paints or coloured crayons

1. Choose your design – you could use the bull below or other Minoan favourites, such as dolphins, lilies or birds.

2. Use a pencil to trace round the picture you choose. Transfer your tracing on to the strip of card. Repeat the process until you have several figures in a row.

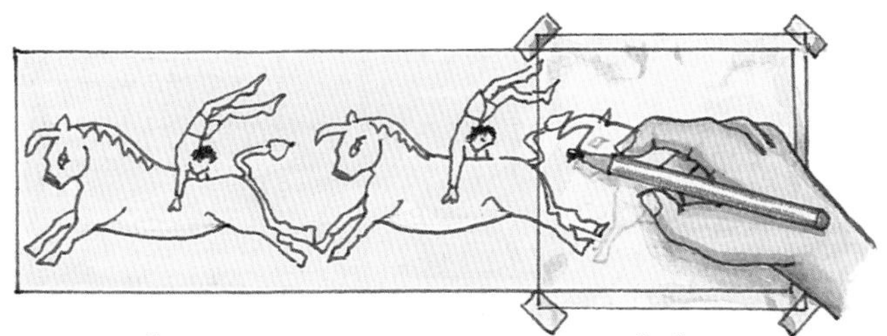

3. Colour in your pictures and the background.

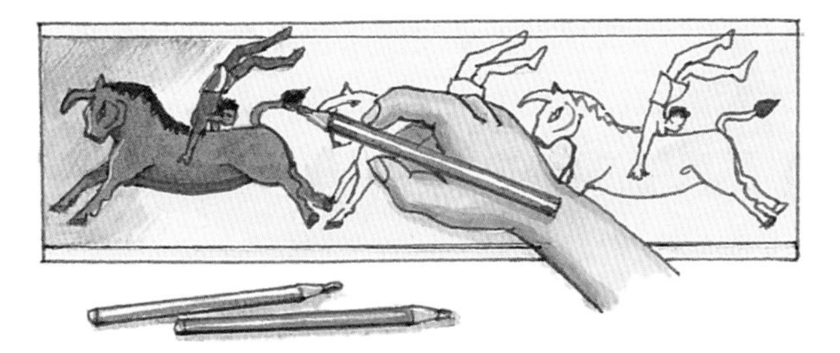

4. Put up your pictures on your bedroom wall.

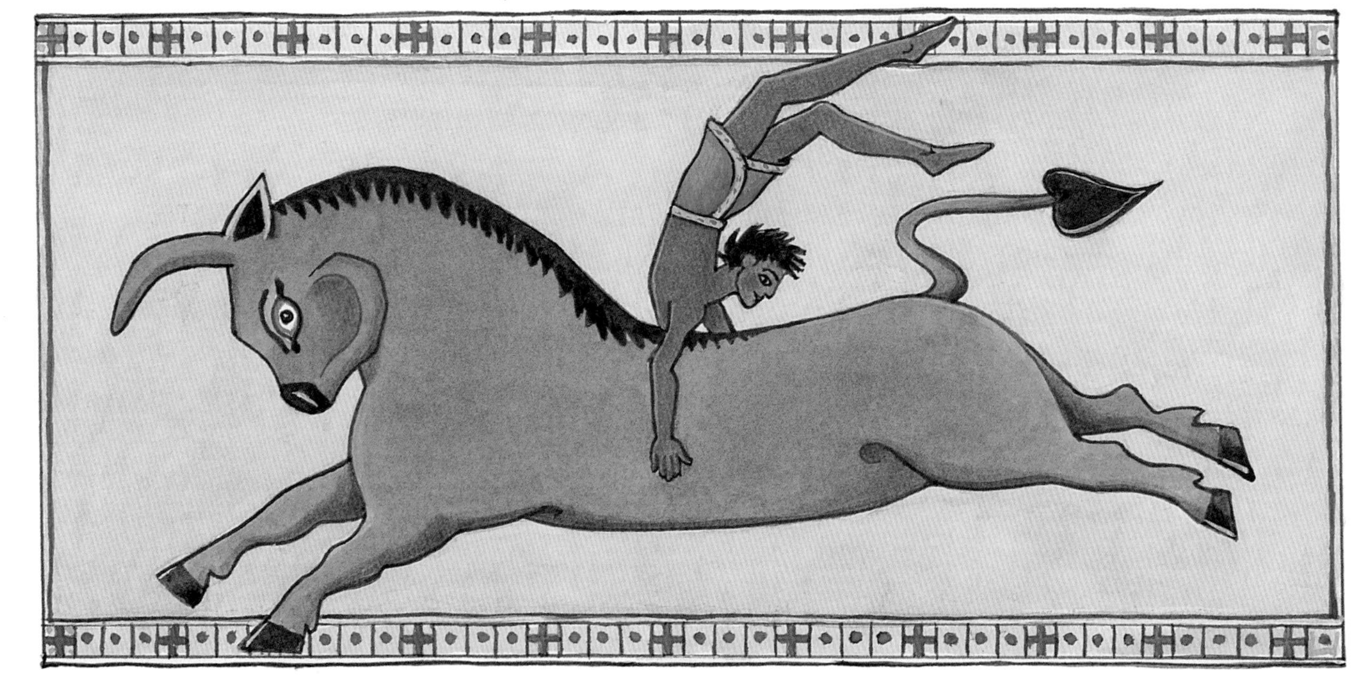

A banner for a procession

During the festival of the *Panathenaea*, the people of Athens marched in a procession to the Acropolis. Sometimes a ship was rolled along in the procession. The new clothes for Athene, the goddess of Athens, were hung from the mast, like a sail.

The owl was the emblem of Athene. Make a special cloth banner for the procession. Use an old white tea towel or a pillow case for your banner. Make a potato cut design of an owl to decorate your banner.

You will need: • an old white tea towel or pillow case • a large potato • a rounded butter knife • fabric paint

1. Cut the large potato in half. Then cut the owl design shown here into the surface of one half of the potato.

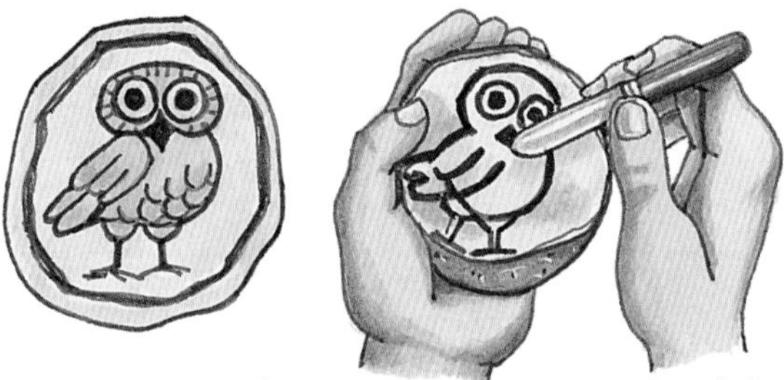

2. Stamp the potato cut into the fabric paint.

3. Smooth out the cloth on a flat surface. Then stamp the potato cut onto the cloth.

4. Repeat this until the cloth is covered with your owl design.

Entertainment for a dinner party

The Ancient Greeks enjoyed listening to music and poetry at dinner parties. The lyre was a very popular instrument and was used to accompany poetry. After dinner, there were often discussions or debates about important political issues or new ideas.

You and your friends could entertain your family in the style of the Ancient Greeks. Here are some suggestions for the things that you could do.

1. Choose poems that you like, or make up some poems. Learn them by heart.

Choose music to go with the poems. Make sure that the pieces are easy to play on a guitar.

Practise saying the poems out loud while the music is played to accompany the poems.

2. Choose different pieces of music that have parts for woodwind instruments such as a flute or a recorder. You could use a drum, tambourine or small cymbals to provide the rhythm.

Practise the music before you perform for your dinner guests.

3. Stage a discussion or debate. Choose subjects or issues that are important to you and your friends. Note down five main points in favour and five main points against each subject to be discussed.

Choose a friend who disagrees with your points of view. Take turns to argue for and against each point, using the notes you have made.

Invite your guests to join the discussion or debate.

A soldier's shield

Imagine a young *hoplite* arriving home after a long campaign fighting against the Persians. He is welcomed back by his mother and sisters. He hangs up his shield and sword and joins the whole village in dancing and feasting. Design a *hoplite* shield. The originals were made from wood, bronze and leather – but you will have to make do with cardboard!

You will need: • a large sheet of cardboard or featherboard, the thickest you can find • a pencil • sticky tape • poster paints • scissors or craft knife

1. Lay out a large, thick sheet of card or featherboard.

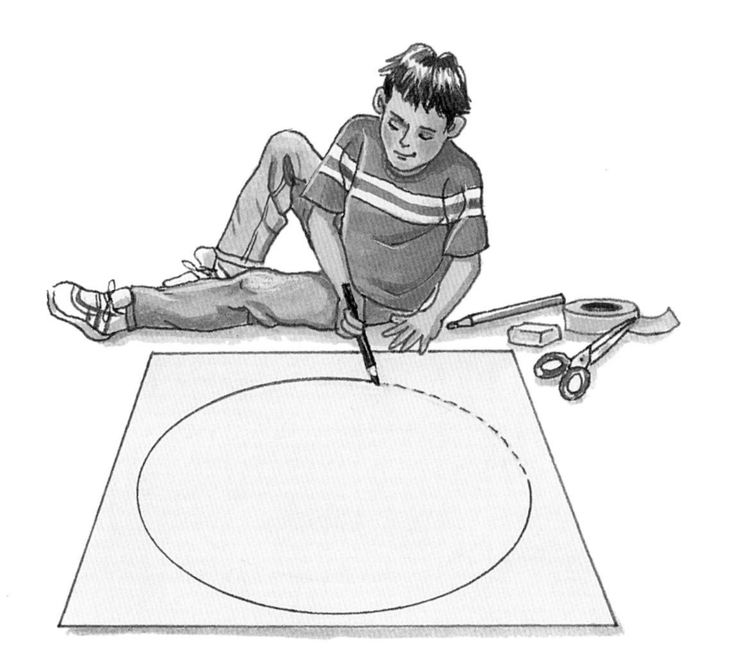

2. Draw a big circle on it, the size of a dustbin lid. Cut out the circle and paint it in a plain colour.

3. Sketch out a shield design, based on one of the designs shown here or make up one of your own.

4. Cut out a piece of the card and stick it to the back of your shield, as an armband.

GLOSSARY

archaeologist: Someone who studies the past by digging up or examining ancient ruins and remains.

capital: The carved block of stone that caps a pillar or column.

citadel: A strongly fortified city or group of buildings.

city-state: One of the small states that grew up in ancient Greece, centred on a single city or island.

colony: A country, or part of one, which another country governs. In ancient Greece a colony was really an overseas settlement.

column: Any large pillar supporting a roof.

comedies: Plays which are funny.

craft: Any trade or pastime in which people use skill to make things by hand.

culture: A people's way of life, including their arts, crafts, customs and beliefs.

democracy: A system of government where the people choose representatives to govern them.

drachma: Greek unit of currency.

earthenware: Pottery made from plain, unglazed clay.

Earth Mother: An Earth goddess, who is believed to create and sustain all living things.

empire: A group of countries which are ruled by a single emperor or government.

excavate: To dig out, especially ancient ruins.

export: To send goods produced in one country for sale abroad.

fibre: A threadlike substance, often taken from plants or animals, mainly used by the ancient Greeks to weave cloth.

flax: A blue-flowered plant, whose tough stems are used to make linen.

fresco: A wall painting made on plaster.

frieze: A long patterned band or picture which is used to decorate a wall.

golden age: The high point in a civilization or culture.

grid: A framework of horizontal and vertical lines sometimes used for town plans .

griffin: A mythical monster, a cross between an eagle and a lion.

import: To bring goods into a country from abroad.

Minoan: Belonging to the civilization that grew up around the palaces of Crete between about 3000 and 1400 BC.

Mycenaean: Belonging to the civilization that grew up around the citadels of southern Greece between about 1900 and 1100 BC.

myrrh: A gum from a tree, used to make perfume.

Peloponnese: The southern section of the Greek mainland, lying below the Isthmus of Corinth.

pendant: A piece of jewellery that hangs on a chain or thong.

potter's wheel: A revolving slab that spins around, helping potters to shape wet clay with their fingers.

sardonyx: A kind of quartz banded with reddish-brown stone.

silhouette: An outline drawing filled in with a solid colour, usually black.

silkworm: A type of caterpillar which spins cocoons of silk.

textiles: Any kind of woven cloth.

tragedies: Plays which are very sad.

warp: The threads which run lengthwise along a piece of woven cloth, hanging down from the crossbar of a Greek loom.

weft: The threads which are woven under and over the warp threads on a loom.

wicks: Long, thin threads put into oil in a lamp, leaving the top end out of the oil, and lit. As the wick burns, it draws up the oil slowly along the thread, so that it continues to burn.

Further reading

Ancient Greece, Anne Pearson, 'Eyewitness' series (Dorling Kindersley, 1992)
Costumes and Clothes, Penelope Paul, 'Legacies' series (Wayland Publishers Limited, 1995)
Food and Feasts in Ancient Greece, Imogen Dawson, 'Food and Feasts' series (Wayland Publishers Limited, 1995)
Greeks, R Wright, 'Craft Topics' series (Watts Publishing Group, 1992)
The Greek News, Philip Steele & Anton Powell (Walker Books, 1996)
The Greeks and Troy, Deborah Tyler, 'Hidden Worlds' series (Zoe Books Limited, 1993)
How would you survive as an Ancient Greek? David Salariya, 'How would you survive?' series (Watts Publishing Group, 1994)
Over 2000 years ago: In Ancient Greece, Philip Sauvain, 'History Detective' series (Zoe Books Limited, 1993)
Technology in the time of Ancient Greece, Judith Crosher, 'Technology in the time of ...' series (Wayland Publishers Limited, 1997)

INDEX